The Children's War and Other Poems

Shaindel Beers' poetry, fiction, and creative nonfiction have appeared in numerous journals and anthologies. She is currently an instructor of English at Blue Mountain Community College in the Eastern Oregon high desert town of Pendleton, and serves as Poetry Editor of Contrary (www.contrarymagazine.com). *The Children's War and Other Poems* is her second collection with Salt Publishing.

Also by Shaindel Beers

A Brief History of Time (Salt, 2009)

The Children's War
and Other Poems

by

SHAINDEL BEERS

SALT

CROMER

PUBLISHED BY SALT PUBLISHING
12 Norwich Road, Cromer Norfolk NR27 0AX, United Kingdom

Salt Publishing 2013

Printed and bound in the United States by Lightning Source Inc

Typeset in Swift 9.5 / 13

ISBN 978 1 84471 930 3 paperback

1 3 5 7 9 8 6 4 2

For the children

Contents

Acknowledgements

Grateful acknowledgment is made to the journals and anthologies in which these poems, some of them in earlier versions, first appeared:

Corium Magazine: *Sometimes the airplanes, From an eight-year-old Darfurian girl's drawing, After a photo of a Chechen girl on a train, After a thirteen-year-old Darufurian boy's drawing, Painting by Azerbaijan War Survivor Sasha Morohov, age 9, Drawing Done by a Child at the Child Rescue Center in Bo, Sierra Leone, January 2002,* and *Painting by a Child at the Landmine Education Center in Dong Ha (Quang Tri Province, Vietnam)*

tinfoildresses: *After a drawing by Mercedes Comellas Ricart, 13, during the Spanish Civil War, After drawings by recipients of the AFSC feeding program in post WWI Europe, After Martija's Watercolor, Croatia, After 16-year-old Kristina's drawing of herself on a beach in Hawaii, Croatia*

The Portland Cello Project has composed music based on: *After 16-year-old Kristina's drawing of herself on a beach in Hawaii, Croatia, Little Amira Honors her Cat, Pepa,* and *After a New York Times article on Balkan Immigrant Children, 6/12/98*

Iron Horse Literary Review: "Love Poem for the Other Woman" and "Azure"

Sententia: "A Prayer for Angel Torres," "For the Boy at the Middle School Poetry Slam, The Dalles, Oregon," and "There Are Men . . . "

The Best American Poetry Blog: "Origins"

The Queen City Review: "Dangerous Games"

The Los Angeles Review: "After *Doctor's Orders*, a fused glass sculpture by Tom Dimond"

Stymie Magazine: "Ode to Plastic Bat and Ball"

Permafrost: "Meditation on Life and Death, August 10, 2008"

Basalt: "Shelly's Daughter Watches the Skateboarders"

Peripheral Surveys: "Nora Evans Brings a Tornado to Holcomb" and "I saw the man who makes the coffins."

Pif Magazine: "The Last Ballet Class Before the Operation" and "The Missing"

Poetry Quarterly: "New Sharon, Iowa"

These Mountains that Separate Us: "The Gift"

Untitled Country Review: "Water, Water Everywhere"

My thanks to Blue Mountain Community College for financing my trips to writers' conferences and workshops to further this work. Thanks to the Oregon Writing Project and the Kenyon Review Writers Workshop, especially workshop leader Carl Phillips, for his inspiring prompts, and to my fellow workshop group members. I am also grateful for funding to go to the AWP annual conference each year and learn from myriad writers there.

Thanks, also, to Molly Fisk, Lisa Cihlar, and Robert Lee Brewer for leading online poetry writing challenges, which inspired many of the poems in this book.

This book wouldn't have been written if it were not for the *Slate.com* article "The Art of War" by Dr. Annie Sparrow and Olivier Bercault, which first inspired me to pursue this project, as well as the countless humanitarians who catalogue and publish artwork done by and about children during war-time. Thank you so much for giving voices to the voiceless. Sources of artwork in book form include

They Still Draw Pictures by Anthony L. Geist and Peter N. Carroll and *Sunflowers in the Sand: Stories from Children of War* by Lisa Curtin.

Love to the entire Salt Family, truly the best publishers on earth. And especially to my "Salt Sister," Terry Ann Thaxton, for her editorial suggestions. Thanks also to Pamela Steele, my Eastern Oregon partner-in-crime for helping to bring poetry to our side of the state.

Lastly, thank you to Jared and Liam, for doing whatever is necessary for us to remain a household of artists. I love you.

The Children's War

I am sure that if the mothers of various nations
could meet, there would be no more wars.

—*E. M. Forster*

Sometimes the airplanes resemble planes;
sometimes they congeal in the distance, like ticks
stuck to the page. Always, the upside down people
are dead. Always, there is a mother screaming.

From an eight-year-old Darfurian girl's drawing

The tank, bigger than the hut, fires
and all of the colors explode from the hut.
Why is this man green?
Because he is from the tank.
Why is this woman red?
Because she was shot in the face.
And why aren't you colored in?
Because it is like I wasn't even there.

After a photo of a Chechen girl on a train

I am four, almost five, and I am beautiful.
I have my red hat, my red coat; I ride
on my mother's lap. People smile at me.
I make them happy. When my mother looks
at them, they look away. My mother has
brown eyes. I have blue. I have only seen
my father in pictures. *We have to practice*
my mother says. *Where are we going?*
To visit Grandma in the country.
What will you do there?
Help Grandma gather eggs and be brave
even if the hens peck me.
Ride Doishka, the pony. I look out the window
at the wildflowers speeding by.
And you mustn't cry says mother *if we get there
and there is no Grandma, no pony.*

After a thirteen-year-old Darfurian boy's drawing

Women flee from their houses as smoke rises
like terrible angels and men in green herd them
like cattle. *What are the men doing to the women?*
Forcing them to be wives. Their houses are gone.
Yes, when you are thirteen,
to be a wife is having a house, a man.
But he is right; the women with the soldiers
are warm and brown; their hair flies around them
as they run. The women who will not be wives
are outlines, uncolored, upside down
in the foreground.

After a drawing by Mercedes Comellas Ricart, 13, during the Spanish Civil War

The plane drops a single black tear of a bomb
that tears a hole in the mountains. The station
bell is mute next to the air raid sirens, and we run,
leaving our bags at the station. Papá reaches for me;
Mamá reaches for Pilar, and we run, never quite grasping
hands, never quite touching. It is a ghost train, light grey
and see-through because we never got on. I didn't finish
the tracks because I never learned where they would go.

After a New York Times article on Balkan
Immigrant Children, 6/12/98

Today is the family tree project. Alana and Danielle share
the green and brown crayons; they are starting with a real tree.
Danielle draws the trunk while she has brown; Alana draws
leaves while she has green, then they switch. *What color
do you want, Leonela?* they ask. That is me. *Black,* I whisper.
Alana wrinkles her nose, slides the crayon bin down the long
table. That is Alana; she doesn't touch colors she doesn't like.
I do not draw a real tree; I do a diagram like in our book.
Rectangles and names. Dad. Mom. Yasmine. Me.
We have birthdates. Renata. Marija. Stjephan. Jadranko. Branimir.
Dead. Dead. Dead. Dead. Dead. I watch the clock while the others
color. It is black and white like my chart; like war.

After drawings by recipients of the AFSC feeding program in post WWI Europe

The women who cook for us are friendly giants,
like the wife in Jack and the Beanstalk. They stir giant pots,
ladle soup into bowls. The counters in the kitchen are stacked high
with rolls. *Essen, essen!* they say. These might be the only words
they know in our language. *Quäkerspeisung.* This means they are here
to feed us. We write poems about the milk they bring.
Each child receives two cups a day
and daily puts on weight that way.
They are to feed us first, but I have made a drawing
of my father eating. When he thought no one was looking,
he put down his spoon, his roll. He picked his soup bowl up
and licked it like a dog. Thick soup is so good after a war.
I did not want to embarrass him, so I drew his eyes looking over—
there. But what of their husbands, these women?
Are they the giants who would make bread of our bones?

After Martija's Watercolor, Croatia

There are things that can happen that you can't draw.
A soldier ripping off the baby's diaper and slamming him
into the wall because it will be easier if the baby
cannot cry. Your mother without a head. You paint splotches.
Green and blue are peaceful. That was before.
Now, everything is red. The red mixed with the green
becomes a sickening brown. The brown that covered
your thighs when the soldier was done with you.

After 16 year-old Kristina's drawing of herself on a beach in Hawaii, Croatia

I will walk the beach and be mysterious in my red dress,
red comb in my hair; two thin, gold necklaces encircling
my neck. I will carry yellow flowers every day. *Something
they will say is different about that girl. Is it her blue eyes?*
They will not see that the war has covered me with a shawl
of sorrow. That I stay outside so buildings will not fall on me.
That I don't have a husband because I don't want him to make
war on me. On my family. Like my father did, turning the guns
right at Zemunik, just another sergeant following orders.

Little Amira Honors Her Cat, Pepa

Fourteen in hiding in a basement
and we all need something to protect.
The men guard the door, the women guard
the children. Grandma holds me, and I hold
Pepa. Pepa himself was love. So when I draw
him, his face is an orange heart. He is smiling
with his mouth and his eyes and his whiskers.
He wears a blue flower as a collar. When
the grenade blew open the shelter, the world
became only Lejla and me. No Mama, no
Grandma, no Jusuf, no Pepa. No Pepa.
I draw Pepa over and over. No one else
because he was mine to take care of.
When I grow up, I will own a pet store.
I will have ten cats named Pepa.
I will do a better job because
I will be bigger.

Painting by Azerbaijan War Survivor
Nighar Aliyeva, age 9

The woman could be any mother out walking
a baby in the cool, night air, hoping the twelve
stars, the moon, will lull him to sleep.
In her blue caftan, her black hijab, she could be
Mary, the mother of Jesus, Fatimah, daughter
of Muhammad. The three bloody men
in the background believe she is one;
the men who shot them believe she's the other.

Painting by Azerbaijan War Survivor
Sasha Morohov, age 9

The Red Cross nurse is smiling and beautiful.
The way I remember my mother in dreams.
The nurse is beautiful because she is not from here.
Nothing here is beautiful any more. Even the sun is sad.
So I did not paint it in the picture. Only its three rays
peek out. Two golden like the sand of Azerbaijan.
One red, like the nurse's lips. Like the cross on her hat.
Her satchel. The sun's rays reach out to touch her. Only her.
The sun does not even see me here, under it, crying.

Drawing Done by a Child at the Child Rescue
Center in Bo, Sierra Leone, January 2002

When the woman asks me "What happened?" I lay out the picture.
Left to right. Left to right. Like we read at school. I put labels
around each scene. *He killed my friend.* I draw the man
with a machine gun. Me with my arms up. My friend lying
on the ground. *The rebel is chasing this boy.* A fast car and a boy
looking out of the picture. Like he is saying "Help!"
He killed the man with a knife. I make sure to make the knife
big. Bigger than both of the men. Bigger than life.
He is burning the house. I use all black, except for the fire
which is red scribble. I wanted page numbers like in our books
at school, but I wasn't sure how because this is one picture,
one piece of paper, four scenes. So I circled numbers. Some
of them are our ages. Some of them are just numbers.

Painting by a Child at the Landmine Education Center in Dong Ha (Quang Tri Province, Vietnam)

We are playing and having fun. All smiling. I have drawn us floating
like we are swimming in the blue sky. Bi`nh is in her pink sweater,
green skirt, and I am in my red dress, red tights. Tuan is laughing
in his blue shirt, red shorts. Above us are skeletons holding
landmines. I don't know yet if they are good or bad. Other children
warning us not to dig in the countryside who learned too late
what not to touch. Or if they are bad spirits tempting us *Go
ahead. Just. One. Touch.* I do know the number I have drawn
on one mine. 13. The number of children lost in our village.

Drawing by a girl named Khitam at the Iraqi Children's Art Exchange

This is a land that could never dream war.
Seven butterflies flit through a peaceful sky.
The trees by the river are so bursting with love
their apples are bright red hearts, a stem sprouting
from each heart's simple cleft. I heard a story once
about a single butterfly's wingbeat starting a hurricane
on the other side of the earth. These are our magic
butterflies, *Emmi*. They will beat the winds of war away
while we camp next to the river. While we live
in the land of my dreams.

After a Photograph of Myrna Tonni showing her drawing at The Iraqi Children's Art Exchange in Amman, Jordan

When we first came to the refugee center, we drew what we knew—
machine guns and soldiers. Shambles of houses.
No, no, said our teacher. *Here, we do not draw sad pictures*
of things like that. This is your new life. A new beginning.
He told us we are going to draw pictures for children
in other countries. We do not want them to think about war.
War is not who we are; it is what has happened to us.
So I draw a princess. How I will grow up to be.
My hair is long and black, I am in a red ball-gown
with purple trim, a purple slip underneath. My eyelashes
are long, like the women on TV. In magazines.
I'm holding a gold fan. I hope a girl in another country
gets my picture. I hope she likes it. I hope she
grows up to be a princess, too. But bigger than me
is the heart I send to the girl oceans away.

After In Memory of the Czech Transport to the Gas Chambers by Yehuda Bacon, Age 16

My father's face rises
out of the crematorium
like a terrible jack-in-the-box,
but he is too exhausted to arc
over the camp yard,
scattering cowering guards
with each bounce. Instead,
he wears the face I last
saw on him—worn down,
defeated. Bags under his soulful
eyes. A scar across the bridge
of his broken nose. A man
who was dead
before they had a chance
to kill him. To mark the moment
of his body's death, I write
10.VII.44, 22:00, in the corner
where an artist's signature
should be.

After "El niño en la colonia" by Jesús Ezquerro Ruiz, Age 10, Residencia Infantil No. 1Onteniente (Valencia)

With fifty children in the colony, playtime is busy.
There is fútbol for the boys and jump rope for girls
and watching the turtles who swim in the fountain.
We have named them. We tell them apart by the marks
on their shells. The teachers remind us to be grateful
for everything. For the wheat bread and milk we have
at every meal. Sometimes we pick flowers for our teachers
to show them we are grateful for having the children's colonies
to keep us safe from the war. For having our teachers
while we cannot have parents. I drew a border to keep
us safe until our parents come back for us. I hope
they can find us across the borders. Because the sun
is so high, he can see us playing and the war,
so I knew not to make him smiling the way that I used to.

After "Evacuación" byMargarita García, Age 10, Residencia Infantil No. 23, Biar (Alicante)

"I noticed that . . . many of the mothers had tears in their eyes. How strange, I thought, how strange. Of course, it wasn't long before I found out why they were crying. They had proposed that those who wanted could send their children out of Madrid . . ."

from an interview with ALFONSO ORTUÑO

The streets are lined with crying mothers and little children.
Children younger than four stay with their families.
Those over fourteen are now grown-ups displaced by war.
The truck with the red flag and *Evacuación* painted
on the side comes to pick up the rest of us. My mother
turns away from me so I cannot see her tears while I wave
from the back of the truck with the other crying children.
Some of the smallest ones do not cry. They think
this is an adventure. Some of them are dressed up
like they are going to a party. Their shoes are shined,
and they wear bows in their hair. Their mothers
shout excitedly from the street, pretending not to be sad.
But I know. I know their hearts are breaking.
They are watching their children being scattered
like a broken strand of brightly colored beads.

After a Spanish Civil War Watercolor, Unknown Artist. Unknown Locale.

Mother shakes her fist at the planes that are bombing
our town. *Pavas!* Mother and I both yell. That's
what we call them. The German airplanes skim
over the village like awkward black turkeys.
Smoke billows from what used to be homes.
Father is hunched under a sack like a beggar.
In the distance, others have loaded a cart
with their belongings. Their dog follows,
ever loyal, barking excitedly. How nice
it would be to be a dog. Everything would be
an adventure. Even the lone tree on the plain
leans away from the village, like it, too,
is trying to flee. We hope against hope
that someday we will return, but the night
that is coming is so dark. How will we ever
find our way?

Other Poems

Me Llamo

for Esteban Guerra

The moment the boy realized his name meant *War*
the moon hid behind a cloud, so he practiced
singing her silver face back to him every night
after his mother tucked him in. When Isa ran from him
on the playground, he stopped and sang to her, too.
He swayed, and each strand of his hair became a chorus
of tinkling bells as his song floated to her. He grew kind
toward old women, visiting them after school
with impromptu flowers. He stopped at the market
to carry groceries for the mothers with babies strapped
to their backs. In the street, he helped old men with stubborn
donkeys. Picked up their dropped canes. Refused the coins
they tried to press into his palms. Each day, he saved
bits of his lunch for the stray dogs and cats he would meet.
At Confession, he recited figures from every
war he could find in the encyclopedias his abuela kept
in the front room. *Padre, I killed 500,000 in Spain*
in the 1930s. And 750,000 in the American Civil War alone.
He sobbed diamonds that dropped into the folds
of the priest's robes. He was an odd boy, but his village
was lit by his love. A light golden but faint, not unlike
the moon he had learned to sing back.

Josephine Refuses the Operation

After a line by Stanley Kunitz.

Be patient with my wound—
know that it will not heal.
The heart, like any muscle,

is going to give out. Some day
it will slow—slower—stop.
Mine sooner because it has been beating

so ravenously, because I have loved
so much living this life. I have loved
the river and the heart-shaped leaves

of the catalpa, and the heart-shaped leaves
of the lilac. The crooked, teethed hearts
of the basswood, the linden. The not-quite-

a-heart leaf of the elm. The sad, clefted
heart of the violet. This going, too,
is sweet. I can't stop it. Won't slow

the trajectory of the soul, the body,
over the cleft to the other half
to become the dust of a star.

June 1, 1926 — August 5, 1962

I knew I belonged to the public and to the world, not because I was talented or even beautiful, but because I never had belonged to anything or anyone else.

— MARILYN MONROE

My mother sent me into the world, too fragile—
tall trumpet lily without a stake. Ivy with nothing
but air to cling to. A beefsteak tomato plant
bursting with its own bounty, no cage to hold
me up. I did what I did out of necessity.
Made *them* cling *to me.* And this gives you
the illusion of control, but you have none.
You are only at their mercy. You have to be
what they want you to be. Give only what
they want from you. *If they love you that much
without knowing you, they can also hate you
the same way.*

Daphne Tells of Her Transformation ...

First, the pursuit. The wet raggedness of his breath
on my shoulder. The leap of my heart. Jolt
of my legs beneath me. My stumbles. My flailing.
The wet slip of gravel under bare feet.

The way I knew that running was useless.
How I knew he would catch me. He, the great hunter,
first blessed with quiver and bow
at four-days-old. Killer of the earth-dragon of Delphi.

Before this, Leucippus' cries at the river. His shrieks
while the naiads shredded his body. How they
could have been my cries if Apollo had his way with me.

Instead, I called out, *Help me, Father!*
Destroy this beauty that pleases too well! Then —
my chest tightening around my pounding heart because
of the bark encasing my torso, pain growing through

my arms as they became branches. Veins and arteries,
xylem and phloem; my fingernails, leaves. He
no longer seemed threatening. What could even a god
do to a laurel tree? It was then that I gave him my hand.

The Naiad's Reply

I adore it, the anger of virgins — *The Afternoon of a Faun*

(MALLARMÉ *trans. by* ROGER FRY)

I woke to the eeriness of his slitted pupils tracing our bodies,
nudged my sister, told her as quietly as I could—*Run!* No use.
Our waist-length curls were twisted round his horns.
Hircine stench already mixed with the smell of our fear.
He'd lulled us to sleep with his flute, bound us using
our own hair as ropes. *Locks*, he would later call them.
Too true. Attacked by man and goat at once; his man-self
slick with sweat. Acrid. The goat part of him coarse hair,
all prodding and needing and pain. Cloven hooves bloodying
our legs, strong arms pressing the three of us into one bleeding,
bleating being. I knew it was useless to fight. It was all that he wanted;
instead, I offered my mouth to my sister. Whispered, *Bite. Down.*
Prayed she would close her eyes. Dream of pomegranates. And sun.

Pain: A Tutorial

First, a memory. One painful enough to scar.
To bruise. Your father leaving. Your brother's
death you've blamed yourself for since childhood.
If only you hadn't said, *Fine, then! Leave!* If you
hadn't played with matches. Had watched him
closer down by the river. Now, press slowly
with scalpel or finger the outline of the wound.
Remind yourself daily. A song you used to sing
when you were little. How you would lie
on your backs and make up stories about cloud animals.
The smell of the flowers in Grandma's window boxes
just before—

Find someone who feels designed to fill this void.
You'll know by matching scars. Let him press them,
too. He'll say, *No wonder your father left.*
I wonder how your brother would feel if he were
here. He knows all the tricks. The little places inside you
no one else has ever gone. Pretend this is the pain
you deserve. That this is the closest love there is.
Let him press. Sometimes hold the scalpel yourself.
Let him guide your hand along the contours. He
cuts so beautifully. He's shaping you. You're his
lovely. His beloved. He'll be so lost without you.

What Is Lifted

Tropical storm Debby batters the Southeast,
and near Boston, Julia is waiting for a kidney. A father
in Wisconsin on a whim pulls out a camera and says,
Smile! His daughter beams; his son looks sullen,
and he wonders, a bit forlorn, *How did my and my wife's
bodies create these two children?* Meanwhile, Julia
sits in her apartment. Wonders if a phone call
will come. Her kidney is functioning at 6%. Her life
has become a list of numbers. Counts. Weeks left.
Anyone can say *Someone else will do it. Someone
else will save her. But what if no one does?*
She turns on music. Pours a glass of water. Squeezes
in a lime. She has started calling this her cocktail,
the Julia Special. She was never sardonic before.
Only 29. In another corner of the country, a woman
knows she is the right blood type. In the shower,
she massages her lower back over her kidneys
with the soap-sponge, wonders what the incision
would look like. Wonders what her husband witnessed
when the boat of the doctor's cupped hands pulled her son
from another incision. But this is another question she is too afraid
to ask. There are so many. The world, so large and frightening
and each of us at its mercy. Each of us, a spirit in a body,
like a child trapped in the womb, a kidney no longer
working. Waiting to emerge, waiting to be replaced,
waiting to be lifted into whatever light comes next.

The Image Grows; It Moves

This is the heart.
Little spark. Pulsating star on the screen.
It is hard to believe someday you will be human.
Right now, you are a blueberry. A kidney bean.

I want to make the world safe for you.
On long walks I snap photographs
so I can show you the flowers that bloomed
while you swirled in the soft bowl of my body. But still,
I'm afraid of being like my parents. How can I keep
from hurting you when violence is the one tool
I have been given?

How will I be ready when we are rushing
toward each other at 160 beats per minute?

Love Poem for the Other Woman

The way sapphires and rubies are both corundum.
The way when we first saw each other, I blurted,
You're beautiful! The way she came with me
to confront him. How he was telling me nonchalantly
that the dog had gotten into the garbage. How his eyes
clouded over when he saw us both there in the kitchen.
I don't have to stay here for this, he proudly puffed,
then, got into the truck with his name painted on the side
and drove away. How we both kept taking him back
despite the danger.

The way I still went to my classroom to teach *King Lear*
after I got her email. The way he accused us of ganging
up on him when we were both Cordelias. The way we never
knew how tight the noose really was. How her daughter
had the name I'd wanted to name a daughter. How she drove
the same car I had wanted to buy. The way when he put
his guns away after doe season he left one bullet out
and said my name was on it. How in the hardware store
when we were looking at hammers, he looked at me and said
One blow is all it would take.

How this could have been a fairy tale with two princesses.
The way no one gets to live happily ever after. The way
she still lives a block away from me. The way she puts
her hand on my shoulder when we run into each other
in the street. How years later, we still feel bewildered.
The way there is no name for what we shared.

The Child-Prophet Grants an Interview

Was Jesus another false Messiah?
Lilies are not tigers.

Whom, then, shall we worship?
A girl will arrive in a butter yellow Subaru, her hair the color
of a new penny. You shall know her by her deeds.

How will her followers find her?
E as in even now, even then.

When is she coming?
The flutter-brush of your eyelashes against your cool pillow will tell you
a July not long from now.

Why has she chosen me?
You have many hearts beating inside you.

Does being chosen mean I have to die?
This flower is beautiful because it is fragile.
You will wake up with the family you had before the volcano.
They have missed you.
You are their only begotten son.

Humiture

In the cheap apartments, the woman
tries to escape the heat. She takes
a Corona from the refrigerator,
presses the lime firm against the bottle's
thin neck, steps into a cool shower,
thinking *Cool inside the body, Cool*
outside the body. Here, the sun
beats down like an hourglass.
Never-ending. Relentless.
Just when she thinks the night
will be cooler, the hourglass
is flipped. The heat ripens the melons
overnight. Concentrates their sugars.
When she lifts the tendrils from her neck,
she sees the salt crystals
she is reduced to. Seven tablespoons
in every human body. Each one
like the lime. The melon.
Every fleshy thing waiting
to be brought to fruition.

A Prayer for Angel Torres

The day I decided to leave so you couldn't call me
a bitch again or say you'd *have to fuck another chick*
if I did something that displeased you Angel Torres
was learning to skip. I know because you told me.
You were putting awnings on a school and the preschoolers
were outside, and you told me how most of the kids
were only managing to gallop, "But this kid, this Angel Torres,"
you said, "He's a really good skipper." You tell me these stories
to melt me. You held out your hand and said, "Here—skip
with me," but I wouldn't. Instead, I hoped for Angel Torres
that there are people who love him. I thought about his brown
eyes and his joy, skipping on that playground. I pictured
an orange sweatshirt, tiny jeans, shoes with some cartoon
character, bounding across the pavement. I mourned
for the childhood of our marriage. The skinny yelled at girl,
the beaten little boy we used to be. I thought of my mother
cowered in corners, my father knocking over furniture,
your four year-old arms spotted with cigarette burns,
your hunger locked in rooms, and how we never escape our past.
I don't know how to pray for us, but this is my prayer for Angel Torres.

For the Boy at the Middle School Poetry Slam, The Dalles, Oregon

When you took the stage, acne-scarred and skinny, I thought it,
but when you read the line about the girl—your girl—being the devil
and paradise at once, and how you'd give anything, not to have
her back, but just for the chance at having her back, I knew
you were one of us. The ones who catch the old hard love.
That forbidden-it's-no-good-for-you-since-the-beginning-of-time-love.
I could feel the, *Oh, no. Another teenage boy love poem at a poetry slam?*
filling the room. But I knew. I wanted to take you aside and tell you,
warn you how no one will understand the thrill you will feel as the mile
markers tick by on an all night drive to see her, how some day
when you know she doesn't love you, you will lie there, awake,
wishing love into her, telling yourself, *If I just wish it enough,
she'll feel it and wake up, right now.* And when she doesn't,
you'll wish again—*Right now.* And then, you'll know that it isn't
like Peter Pan and believing in fairies, but you'll keep trying.
Your friends will wait for you to grow up, but this isn't a condition
you grow out of. It's a condition you grow into. An evolution.
I have been the crying girl at dances, the woman sobbing
in the arms of the other woman, the one clutching a funeral program.
The secret? Don't change a thing. Your friends will try
to stop you. They'll tell you, you need to build up walls. Protect
your heart. These are the parts we don't have. You were born with that old
hard love that's like sidearming your heart into a brick wall
every time, and you won't learn, but, trust me, you don't want to.
Your friends will have marriages that last. Babies. And mortgages.
You might even be jealous. You'll try to tame that old hard love
of yours, like chaining a wolf in the backyard. Your friends
with their diapers and laundry will whisper about you at night,
talk about how to get you help. Pity them lying next to one another,
talking about you. That's not love. That's not even living.

Dark-haired girl in the park—

The coffee stirrer he bobs in his lips
is the same pink as the kalanchoe
you potted in first grade for your mother
on Mother's Day.
His eyes are the blue of millefiori paperweights
you marveled at on the museum fieldtrip
when you were twelve.

Different synapses would spark
if it were a cigarette
or a toothpick
or if his eyes were brown,
but right now,
you are fifteen, and you don't know this.

Your parents are trying to stop you
because they don't want to lose you,
but they don't see that they
don't even belong to themselves
but to mortgages
and taxes
making ends meet
and putting food on the table.
They don't remember love like this;
only its crushing absence
when it ends.
Which it will. But please
don't believe that, either.
You are too young and too beautiful
to imagine such tragedies as the breaking
of your own heart.

Your parents have been weighed down
by life, by worry
for you and your brother,
by the closings of factories and stores.
If you were a different sort of girl,
they would be worried
by the stock market or shareholders,
and they would
still be trying to stop you.
Don't let them.
He will be waiting for you
on the swings
at the park at three.
On your porch, like a starved dog,
the days when your father works late.
Go to him.
Now.
Never again will you be so beautiful,
so needed.

There Are Men ...

Who are at once scalpel and salve.
They have only one spigot for honey or gasoline,
and you don't know which you will get until it hits
your tongue. Sip slowly. Protect the soft palate.
They will whittle you until you become
the loneliest statue on the planet. Some days
this will make you feel special and singular.
Your pedestal will be dizzying. When you
and the other muses lean toward one another,
some of you will shatter. This is to be expected;
this was always the plan. There will be more of you;
there always are, always have been.

Origins

My parents were lonely geniuses.
I found their letters to each other in a plastic bag,
my twentieth year, when my mom was in jail,
and I was trying to sort out the life they'd given
my siblings and me. *You were the smartest person
I'd ever met* they'd each written to the other.
But they couldn't function like other parents.
It was all yelling and name-calling
and eventually knives and guns. And I grew up,
wondering where smart would get you.
But it always seemed better than the alternative—
my friends, whose parents had plenty of love
but no books, no imagination, a limited vocabulary
with which to rip out the heart of the beloved.

Dangerous Games

Those hot summer days, no one ever checked where we were.
The air was so heavy, adults couldn't be bothered with kids;
children were not to be seen or heard until the coolness of sunset
settled in. We were supposed to stay outside, amuse ourselves.
We built a ramshackle tree house that could have killed us any minute.
Scraps of wood, a rope to help us up the side of the oak that I was always
afraid to scale. Afternoons, we'd nap in the pop-up camper between
the riding mower shed and the garage in our child-sleep
uniforms of undershirts and briefs after we'd exhausted ourselves
with stories and games. I'd lie on the rough upholstery and kick
my legs in the air, chanting, *Suffocate! Suffocate! Suffocate!*
and you'd press the pillow over my face. Early on, I'd panic and pummel
and this was the game, learning to fight you off, but then I practiced
acceptance, letting the pillow replace everything else I might need,
sinking under, just to the brink, the stillness of black and of blue.

Partly Cloudy

Even since she was a little girl, she has wondered
why the weatherman says "partly cloudy," because
isn't it also "partly sunny"? And she isn't from glass-
is-half-full-people. She knows like any full-hipped woman
that a rising up is first pushing into the earth, the sinking
before the attempt at flight. And so, she is partly in wonder
when she sees the tractor driving itself across the field,
partly panicked when the parti-colored border collie
is crying at the door. When she finds him, his lips are
partly blue, his face, partly ashen. She holds him there
in the sandy loam earth as the tractor stops in a gulley.
That night, a neighbor comes and offers to plow the partly
furrowed field. Three days later, he is buried on a partly
cloudy day. When she drops the first handful of soil
onto the mahogany coffin, she is partly distraught,
partly at peace.

Routine

Each night, in front of the mirror, she starts
with her eye make-up, because there is so much.
Cotton discs pile up in the trashcan next to the sink
still white at the edges, black in the middle, mascara
smudged with whichever color shadow shaped the contours
of her upper lids. Then cheeks. Two brown cotton rounds
float down into the tulip-shaped bin. She is slowly becoming
the self she used to be. Before she steps into the shower,
she pulls her hair up, loose pony-tail looped into a knot so
the water can touch her directly. Steam its way into her.
She will wash her hair last. Some nights it smells like smoke;
other nights, Old Spice, weed. She puts her left foot on the side
of the tub, ceramic cool and smooth in her arch; she takes
the shower head between her legs, spreads herself
to the spray, rinses the last four hours away.

If Tesla Had Aimed His Death Ray at Vortex, Kentucky

There wouldn't be a girl at Target in her red polo shirt
and khakis, waiting for a boy in a Ford Ranger
who will drive up, steady as an assembly line,
singing Garth Brooks' "Friends in Low Places,"
to pick her up from work. She would not stretch
like a lily on a stem, straining for the sun, to see if he is there,
in the indigo pick-up to rescue her from shoppers
too good for Wal-Mart who will let you know it
by unleashing a storm of insults the way Wal-Mart shoppers
are too meek to. When she gets in, he will change
from Garth Brooks to The Beatles out of respect,
and they will sing off-key about the octopus's garden.
They will joke about getting a van and painting it
like a yellow submarine. You are happy for them,
Dear Reader, because you know that death is stalking them
like a panther. Time does not stretch like Turkish Delight,
and you are glad that Tesla did not aim his death ray
at Vortex, Kentucky, because these are your parents.
The quiet trailer park girl, the burly boy in the pick-up.

Clean

What no one understands is that it feels like you have swallowed
your guardian angel. She is beautiful and blue-eyed and is swimming
through your veins, massaging the nuclei of your every cell. She knows
all those little tricks not even a lover knows—how to play
your favorite aria in your heart, how to make your brain thrum
the chords of Dvorak or Ravel. The more you want her, the more
she drifts just out of reach. And now, everyone is asking you to stop
needing her, telling you she is just an illusion, but she is more real
than anything you have ever felt before. She is the center of a daffodil
just opening, the light splintered through an ice covered branch, everything
that reminds us we want to live through the winter. And everyone wants
you to never call on her again. You can give up this angel, little girl.
There will be others. None so sweet but many less cruel. You will want
to die, but you won't. While she is in your head, you are not
your own. The Dvorak is discordant and the Ravel will crescendo forever,
but you won't know it. You won't know until years after she is gone how
close this dark angel came to flying you away forever.

The Baby

The baby, not understanding he was only
supposed to nap for a few hours, forgot
and became a seed. The warmth of the chick
yellow blanket caused his toes to sprout first.
By mid-March, his nose would begin to blossom.
His roots plunged through the particle board bottom
of the designer crib his parents spent too much money on.
When he grew through the ceiling of the little bungalow
on Third Street, his mother became a bird.
His father, however, was an accountant
and could not even imagine being an art history
professor. Some people are incapable of change.
His mother liked to collect lost hair from
the young girls of the neighborhood to build
silky nests. Sometimes she would steal
ribbons, a silver gum wrapper. Her nests
were beautiful. Her chicks hatched and were
always hungry, pink mouths. One day, one
dreamt he was a baby.

The Little Girl

The little girl, wanting to grow big,
ate everything on her plate. She started
with the vegetables, which would get cold first,
then, the macaroni and cheese, which was her favorite.
Next, were the three fish sticks. Then, her miniature
fork. The pink peonies in the centerpiece,
and the vase made by her mother's boyfriend,
the ceramics teacher. The table needed to be
disassembled, but she had watched it be put together,
and she had a keen mind. Keen enough to take apart
anything from IKEA, at least. Next, the dining room
walls and the front door. The porch railing went down easier
after she placed a juicebox on her tongue, enjoying the cherry
burst when she chomped it. Then, Mrs. Robbins from next door
who was supposed to call her mom if anything seemed amiss.
Poor Mrs. Robbins who just stopped by to say,
"Angie. Hi, Angie Dear. I just wanted to make sure
everything was okay—"

After Doctor's Orders, a fused glass sculpture, by Tom Dimond

The man with the birdhead fingertips
feeds all the baby birds. He walks by gooseberries,
elderberries, his beak fingers clicking away.
He scans trees. Haunts skylines. Phonelines.
Searches for pink mouths. Tiny sharp tongues
to drop the berries onto. He knows only
three hundred more birds to feed, and he will
become one. He knows his bones are hollow.
He has felt the southern pull on him in fall,
the northern tug in spring. The feathers
are sprouting out of the wingbones in his back.
One day he will no longer be able to call in sick
to work. All that will come out is a squawk.
A caw. No one at the office will notice
when he soars away overhead. They will think
the enormous shadow just a trick of light,
another pigeon shitting on their concrete building.

Ode to Plastic Bat and Ball

Plastic bat and ball, I loved you. You made
me different. Not like all the other girls.
I could hit the ball out of the yard, over the fence,
and we'd call it a home run. "Over the fence! Over
the fence!" I'd chant, and Dad would hit it over
whenever I wanted. When I got taller, I didn't even
use the gate. I'd leap the fence, pick up the ball,
and rifle it back. Catcher flies up
for hours. That welling hope of catching
the ball to be up next—because batting
was the most fun. All the attention on me
at the plate. I would stand in my left-hand
batting stance until I felt molded there—a statue—
right out the back door. Later, I learned cruelty,
throwing the stinging plastic ball at my sister,
yelling at her when she couldn't catch.
But you made me who I was, plastic bat and ball. You
made me the hero of the boys. The one girl who could
hit it out of the yard, every single time.

II.

Plastic bat and ball, you were with me when I learned
life's meanest lesson. That to be a girl and smaller
is always worse. In the park, I'd play with whoever wanted.
Andy and his family or anyone there on a picnic.
Under the pavilion where I learned to read bad words
on the rafters, two boys took you away — plastic bat
and ball. Big, hulking boys. Larger than my father
who could hit the ball out of the yard whenever
he wanted. The sandy-haired one held the bat up
to my face and said, "There's a part of a man like this."
He thrust the bat closer. My face flinched at the cold coming off
of it. He said, "It gets hard like this." Shook the bat closer.
"Someday, you will want it up inside you." The other boy
laughed. Then one of them, I don't remember, unzipped
and peed a puddle under the picnic table. Swished
the business end of the bat in it, rolled my ball through,
then told me to go home. I knew then, boys like this,
they were the kings. This was their world.
And I was only visiting.

Meditation on Life and Death, August 10, 2008

That day the boundary between life and death was present
but not clear. My cats had brought a mouse
onto the porch. Its tiny grey body grizzled, its paws clenched
into tight little fists. I knew it was dead.
But more than once, looking out onto the deck
I thought I saw it move, until I recognized its twitching
as the landing and taking off of flies from its body.
Their abandonment and return. That same day you
decided to keep your wife from leaving you ever again.
You called her to the house one last time, maybe
to pick up something she'd left behind, to sort out arrangements
for the children. And then, you shot her and then yourself.
That night, I shouldn't have but listened to the 9-1-1 call.
Her cries to the dispatcher, *There's so much blood everywhere.*
I'm so scared. I don't want to die. At the end, everything
becomes a plea. I recognized the tone in my voice once,
how I was sure, sinking into anesthesia, that I wouldn't
come out. I panicked and cried the same way, *I don't want*
to die over and over again, begging the doctor to hold
my hand until I was gone somewhere inside my own body.
What I am struggling with is this—that you could sing
a love song sweeter than any boy in the choir. You would
lean against the piano and our hearts would fall open. Now,
I know, even then, you understood more than anyone
about leaving—how every journey, no matter how planned,
we each have to go alone.

Shelly's Daughter Watches the Skateboarders

She stands transfixed on the sidewalk,
beatific—a picture of seven-year-old devotion.
Her face follows them like sunflowers charting
the sun as they rumble down our street, kings
in their teenaged manginess. I'm only driving by,
but I want to stop the car and tell her to *Get inside*
right now. Those boys want nothing to do with you.
I want to tell her *Even when you are old enough to look*
at boys like that, it will come to no good. They
will be like children, waiting for a present, brimming
with goodness on Christmas Eve, and then, when it is time
for The Opening of Gifts they will not peel tape back slowly,
admire the matched lines of Christmas wrap someone
so carefully fretted over. It will be a carnage of tissue
paper, a despondent pile of bows. Get inside now,
bury yourself in the soft flannel of Princess sheets,
the safety of canopy bed. Hold your breath and lie flat
against the mattress. Stay hidden for all of us.

Nora Evans Brings a Tornado to Holcomb

Like any Kansas girl raised on a vengeful,
Old Testament God, she'd tried to be "good"
but six months together, and Brady leaving
for college in the fall made prom night seem
almost like waiting... So, how
was she supposed to know as the dress
caressed her hips, her thighs, her calves,
before it pooled on the teal Holiday Inn carpet,
that the tornado was penciling its way toward town,
carving a path as precise as the angel of death
over Egypt. The Johnsons' farm untouched
except for a trench through the east forty of wheat,
but the McKinnerney's Jersey calf, Butterscotch,
would be found impaled two miles over on Keller's
cedar tree. All of Sixth Street gone except
for The Mane Event hair salon and a baby,
mysteriously, unharmed, set down on the o yard line
of the football field, and she, Nora Evans,
not even the prom queen, but just a girl,
had caused it all?

I saw the man who makes the coffins.

—a borrowed line from Camille Norton

I saw the man who makes the coffins.
I watched him appraise everyone
at the street fair—the man selling corn dogs
who would take an oversized. The small girl
walking her dog who would take a Child45H
with light pink velvet interior and her dog
who would probably just be buried under
a maple tree in a backyard, so unlike
the Egyptians. There were the children
bouncing in the Moonwalk whose bodies
would need to be measured beforehand.
Their joyful squeals, however boundless,
would take up no space. When he talked
to the girl at the organic smoothie stand,
I saw her through his eyes—an eco-coffin—
cardboard, printed with a field of scarlet
poppies, the lid, a summer sky. He smiled
at her though she was the type who would
never give him business. He knew she
wouldn't think it morbid that his solid
poplar box rested on two sawhorses
in the garage next to his Chevy Tahoe.
As he placed his order and she laughed
at his small-talk—the solid pines,
the cherry veneers, the infant angel-
sleepers, the 18 Gauge Steels,
all became alive to him, he took no
notice of us. There was only her,
and the rest of us, the world
of the dead, fell away.

The Last Ballet Class Before the Operation

It is done. The time has come.
She knows she has held out as long
as she possibly can. That there is a limit
to the number of pills you can take in a day
to chase away pain, but this is her last request.
She stands at the barre, black hair sleeked
into a bun, nondescript as the girls in a chorus line.
She tries to make the music block out her thoughts,
This is my last grande-plié in first, my last demi
plié in second, and, elevé, and hold. Her eyes
follow her fingers during port de bras. And now,
onto the floor. When she was a girl, even in
college, floor couldn't come soon enough. Now,
it is all moving too fast—*allegro vivace*.
Another day on the coda from *Swan Lake*.
Inside passé turn, step, step, lift—why must the leg
she will not use after tomorrow lead it all?
When the music ends, she realizes they
have been watching her. The sea of girls has
parted and stopped, and she has been dancing
a solo. It is as if something magic has happened.
She has not told them. She will not. She will say,
I don't have the time anymore—
My son—
She might not have to say anything. It is a big
city; there are many dancers. No one might
even notice.

New Sharon, Iowa

Every time I passed the sign, I wished there was a town
for each of us so we could swing off the interstate, into a slower
way of life and pick up the us we'd always meant to be —
the one who'd gone to the right school, who worked industriously
each day, the one who knew how to say no to chocolate cake.
It would be the strangest thing; she would be just like you
but better. The quandary — how long would it take
for everyone to notice? Oh, how mad you'd be if right away,
everyone was asking what'd you'd done — found religion,
gotten laid, come into unexpected money. But, of course,
you wouldn't know; they'd be asking new you who would
smile sweetly, nod appreciatively, maybe even laugh flirtatiously
while old you sat somewhere, in a processing plant, fretting
that maybe it wasn't such a good idea to take that exit,
the New in front of your name looked so inviting,
you thought you'd be adventurous just this once
and, besides, what could go wrong in a town
of only thirteen hundred?

The Gift
(for my Golden Eagles)

My students at the rez school carry their toughness
like currency. On Facebook one senior says he's
a 6'6" badass Native American. The students work
their way around the "No Swearing in Class" rule
by saying *What the F? You're so full of S.* The day
I ask the class, *What would you ask the author*
if he were here, the normally quiet but smart girl says,
I'd ask him, "Are you my father? Because
I've never met that bastard in my life."
We all laugh because it's the most honest answer
that can be given. We laugh because honesty
is uncomfortable here in this trailer where I'm
supposed to lie to these high-schoolers, tell them
if they work hard enough, they can be anything.
The way the lie was told to me. We laugh because
we're all in this together—our falling apart houses
and cars and hearts and lives. I wish I could tell them,
The thing that you have is this. The vastness.
The peacocks in the middle of the road, the man playing
air guitar as he walks along Mission Highway.
And I know, Children, that this isn't much, but it's the gift,
the one gift, these stories, that can't be taken away.

The Missing

She wants it to be the way it used to be
but it isn't. Anything could set her off.
The sunlight hitting the field a certain way
a gentle swaying of the wheat. The way
Dolly warbles on a *Country Hits of the 1970s*
album. The way the dog suddenly starts at
a sound no one else hears. It has been eight
years since he got on the school bus at the end
of the gravel drive and was never seen again.
The tick mark on the kitchen doorway records
him as 46" forever. When she held the ruler
level above his head, he'd laughed, *Maybe
next year I'll be taller than you!*
I bet when you're twelve, she'd said,
then gone back to stirring. If he is out there,
how tall is he? Have his shoulders broadened?
Would she even know him if she saw him?
Josh is missing, too. He goes days
without uttering more than a syllable.
Sometimes she acts like she hasn't heard
him, so he has to repeat himself, so she
can pretend he talks to her more, even
if it is just, *Can you please pass the salt?*
She wants to know where inside of himself
he goes when he plows the lazy contours
of their farm, when he is in town buying
dog food and diesel. She has been painfully
present for all of it—the police searches,
the interviews, and now the loneliness—
the loneliness.

Water, Water Everywhere

When he tells you he needs you like he needs air,
you're tempted to fall back on telling him you need him
like water. But water is something you've always been
afraid of. Since the lake with the slippery bottom,
since the slick pondweed wrapped itself around your
ankles and you choked, sputtered, choked, flailed,
felt the entire lake pushing itself into your lungs.
Resist this temptation. You need him like the flowers
need the sun, and you know, more than anyone,
that where air is, water is not.

I wish I was Tiger Lily — the idea of true self concept

I would thrust myself through soil in monocot defiance.
Strain to touch the sun. Unfurl a bold orange tongue
to taste the world. Everything a pushing, a furthering of me.
Six stamens, one pistil, lithe style, three lobed-stigma.
Everything about me orange and sex. Purple brown freckles
dazzling you to my center. The Indian princess who will
not give Peter Pan up. A knife in the mouth. Silent
even when drowning. No comforting nursery to save
me. No Nana. No Lost Boys. No pixie dust. No starstuff.
Just me and me and me. And that is more than enough.

Azure

From the orange hammock of his stroller, Liam squeals,
throws his hands up. We realize he is trying to grab

the vastness. *That's the sky*, we say. He squeals again,
his hands opening and closing, tiny white flowers

against a bright blue field. How magical, like the ancients
who thought the stars were holes in the dome above us,

a way for the gods to keep watch over humanity.
How like a god he is, being wheeled along the shaded sidewalk,

grasping even the dizzying sky in his tiny fists,
as we, his servants, name everything brought before him.

This is the house of yearning —

the featherbed on rusted box springs.
The cobwebbed windows,
a milk bottle vase on the sill.
The way the cottonwoods shade the shed
that is no longer there. The husband
and wife smile young and hopeful
from a dusty frame on the dresser.
This is the cradle that held their daughter.
The stove where the wife baked their bread.
The mudroom where he pulled off
his boots every night after milking.
This is the part where you realize every
broken window is a piece of you.

Notes

Introductory poem
http://www.columbia.edu/cu/lweb/eresources/exhibitions/children/
　　html/55.html

From an eight year old Darfurian girl's drawing http://www.slate.com/
　　id/2122730/slideshow/2122122/

After a photo of a Chechen girl on a train
http://www.coriummagazine.com/wp-content/uploads/2010/03/beer-
　　sphoto.jpg
(Photo originally at http://hrw.org)

After a thirteen year old Darfurian boy's drawing
http://www.slate.com/id/2122730/slideshow/2122122/fs/0//
　　entry/2122113/

After a drawing by Mercedes Comellas Ricart, 13, during the Spanish Civil War
http://www.columbia.edu/cu/lweb/eresources/exhibitions/children/
　　html/22.html

After a New York Times article on Balkan Immigrant Children, 6/12/98
http://tv.nytimes.com/learning/general/specials/kosovo/article6.html

After drawings by recipients of the AFSC feeding program in post WWI Europe
https://afsc.org/category/topic/germany

After Martija's Watercolor, Croatia
From *Sunflowers in the Sand: Stories from Children of War* by Leah Curtin

After 16 year-old Kristina's drawing of herself on a beach in Hawaii, Croatia
From *Sunflowers in the Sand: Stories from Children of War* by Leah Curtin

Little Amira Honors Her Cat, Pepa
From *Sunflowers in the Sand: Stories from Children of War* by Leah Curtin

Painting by Azerbaijan War Survivor Nighar Aliyeva, age 9
http://azer.com/aiweb/categories/magazine/23_folder/23_articles/23_
childrensart.html

Painting by Azerbaijan War Survivor Sasha Morohov, age 9
http://azer.com/aiweb/categories/magazine/23_folder/23_articles/23_
childrensart.html

*Drawing Done by a Child at the Child Rescue Center in Bo, Sierra Leone,
January 2002*
http://allafrica.com/photoessay/sl_drawings/photo3.html#photo

*Painting by a Child at the Landmine Education Center in Dong Ha (Quang Tri
Province, Vietnam)*
http://www.vietvet.org/artsofwar/leelee.htm

Drawing by a girl named Khitam at the Iraqi Children's Art Exchange
http://iraqichildrensart.org/contact.html

*After a Photograph of Myrna Tonni showing her drawing at The Iraqi
Children's Art Exchange in Amman, Jordan*
http://iraqichildrensart.org/press/get_the_children_home.pdf

After In Memory of the Czech Transport to the Gas Chambers *by
Yehuda Bacon, Age 16*
http://www.english.illinois.edu/maps/holocaust/art.htm

*After "El niño en la colonia" by Jesús Ezquerro Ruiz, Age 10, Residencia Infantil
No. 1Onteniente (Valencia)*
http://libraries.ucsd.edu/speccoll/tsdp/spain/valencia/onteniente/resi6.
htm

After "Evacuación" by Margarita García, Age 10, Residencia Infantil No. 23, Biar (Alicante)
http://www.alba-valb.org/resources/lessons/they-still-draw-pictures-1/leaving-home/Evacuacion.jpg, quote from *They Still Draw Pictures* by Anthony L. Geist and Peter N. Carroll.

CPSIA information can be obtained
at www.ICGtesting.com
Printed in the USA
FSHW011318201218
54603FS